# What's New, B.C.?

Johnny

**CORONET BOOKS**
Hodder Fawcett, London

First published by Fawcett Publications, Inc.
New York 1968

*Coronet Edition 1973*
*Fourth impression 1981*

---

Printed and bound in Great Britain for
Hodder Fawcett Ltd,
Mill Road, Dunton Green, Sevenoaks, Kent
(Editorial Office: 47 Bedford Square, London, WC1 3DP)
by Hunt Barnard Printing Ltd., Aylesbury, Bucks

ISBN 0 340 16881 1

SEE THE FUNNY, FUNNY WALL.

SEE JANE JUMP THE WALL.

JANE HAS DEFECTED.

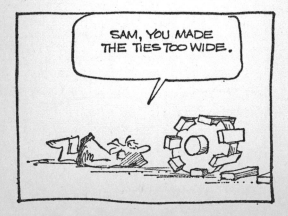

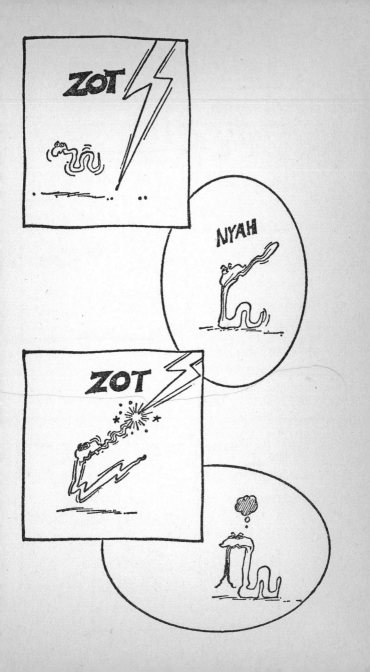

OH, WELL . . .

I GUESS I JUST GO THROUGH LIFE AS A PREHISTORIC ROLLS-ROYCE.

THE TROUBLE WITH THIS WORLD IS: THERE'S TOO MUCH HATRED!

PEOPLE HATE OTHER PEOPLE, ...

ANIMALS HATE OTHER ANIMALS, ...

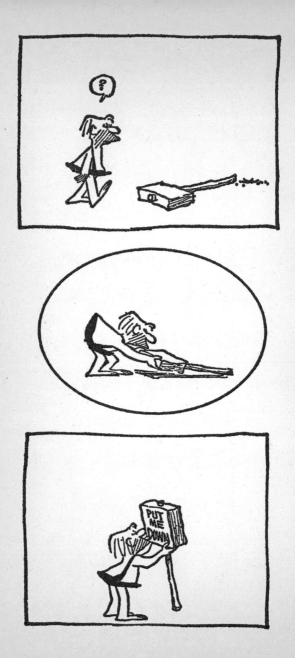